England

by Tracey Boraas

Reading Consultant:
Dr. Robert Miller
Professor of Special Education
Minnesota State University, Mankato

Bridgestone Books
an imprint of Capstone Press
Mankato, Minnesota

Bridgestone Books are published by Capstone Press
151 Good Counsel Drive, P.O. Box 669, Mankato, MN 56002
http://www.capstone-press.com

Copyright 2003 © by Capstone Press. All rights reserved.
No part of this publication may be reproduced in whole or in part, or stored in a retrieval system, or transmitted in any form or by any means, electronic, mechanical, photocopying, recording, or otherwise, without written permission of the publisher. For information regarding permission, write to Capstone Press, Dept. R, 151 Good Counsel Drive, P.O. Box 669, Mankato, Minnesota 56002.
Printed in the United States of America

Library of Congress Cataloging-in-Publication Data
Boraas, Tracey.
　England/by Tracey Boraas.
　　p. cm.—(Countries and cultures)
　　Summary: An introduction to the geography, history, economy, culture, and people of England.
　　Includes bibliographical references and index.
　　ISBN 0-7368-0937-6
　　1. England—Juvenile literature. [1. England.] I. Title. II. Series.
DA27.5 .B67 2003
942—dc21　　　　　　　　　　　　　　　　　　　　　　　　　　　　　2001008374

Editorial Credits
Gillia Olson, editor; Karen Risch, product planning editor; Heather Kindseth, series designer; Heidi Meyer, cover and interior designer; Alta Schaffer, photo researcher

Photo Credits
Adam Woolfitt/CORBIS, 11; Adrian Arbib/CORBIS, 36; Bryn Colton/Assignments Photographers/CORBIS, 63; Capstone Press/Gary Sundermeyer, 53; Chip & Rosa Maria Peterson, 49; Cordaiy Photo Library Ltd./CORBIS, 55; Digital Stock, cover (both), 1 (left, right), 4, 44, 56; Doranne Jacobson, 41; Ecoscene/CORBIS, 8; Geray Sweeney/CORBIS, 32; Graham Bartram, 57 (bottom); GRAHAM TIM/CORBIS SYGMA, 35; Hulton/Archive by Getty Images, 21, 27, 28; Hulton-Deutsch Collection/CORBIS, 46; PhotoDisc, 1 (middle); Photri-Microstock, 15, 31; Photri-Microstock/Jeff Greenberg, 50; Provided by: Audrius Tomonis-www.banknotes.com, 43 (bottom); Ric Ergenbright/CORBIS, 13; Stockhaus Limited, 57 (top); Stock Montage, Inc., 18, 22, 25

Artistic Effects
Digital Stock, PhotoDisc, Inc.

Capstone Press wishes to thank Dewi Williams from the British Consulate-General in New York for his assistance in preparing this book.

1 2 3 4 5 6 07 06 05 04 03 02

Contents

Chapter 1
Fast Facts about England 4
Explore England 5

Chapter 2
Fast Facts about England's Land 8
England's Land, Climate, and Wildlife 9

Chapter 3
Fast Facts about England's History 18
England's History and Government 19

Chapter 4
Fast Facts about England's Economy 36
England's Economy 37

Chapter 5
Fast Facts about England's People 44
England's People, Culture, and Daily Life 45

Maps
Geopolitical Map of England 7
England's Land Regions and Topography 16
England's Industries and Natural Resources 39

Features
English Gardens 15
England's Money 43
Learn British Slang 50
Recipe: Make Treacle Tart 53
England's National Symbols 57
Timeline 58
Words to Know 60
To Learn More 61
Useful Addresses 62
Internet Sites 62
Index 64

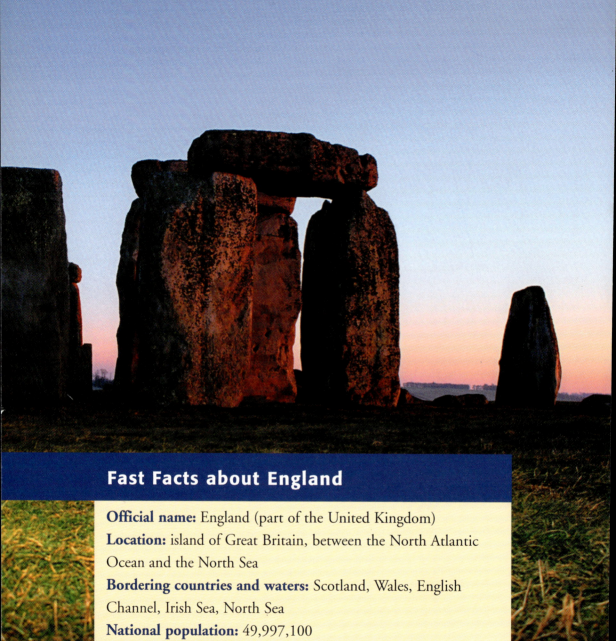

Fast Facts about England

Official name: England (part of the United Kingdom)
Location: island of Great Britain, between the North Atlantic Ocean and the North Sea
Bordering countries and waters: Scotland, Wales, English Channel, Irish Sea, North Sea
National population: 49,997,100
Capital city: London
Major cities and populations: London (7,375,100); Birmingham (1,017,300); Leeds (731,400); Sheffield (531,400); Bradford (489,500)

Chapter 1

Explore England

Stonehenge has fascinated people for hundreds of years. This mysterious structure of giant stone blocks in southern England receives more than 1 million visitors each year. Although no one is certain, experts believe people built Stonehenge in ancient times as a tribal gathering place and religious center.

Archaeologists suggest that Stonehenge was built between 2800 and 1500 B.C. in three separate stages. Over time, people changed the look of Stonehenge. They added to and rearranged the enormous stone blocks. Archaeologists believe the stones originally sat in three rings with two horseshoe-shaped structures in the center.

Only parts of the third ring and horseshoe center remain today. Some of the center stones stand 22 feet (6.7 meters) tall and weigh 30 to 40 tons (27 to 36 metric tons).

◀ Stonehenge was built between 2800 and 1500 B.C.

England

England covers about three-fifths of the island of Great Britain, the largest island of the British Isles. The British Isles include Great Britain, Ireland, and several smaller islands. The English Channel runs along England's southern border, and the North Sea forms England's eastern border. Wales and the Irish Sea border England to the west. Scotland runs along England's northwestern border.

Although England is very small, it is one of the most densely populated countries in the world. England covers a total area of 50,333 square miles (130,362 square kilometers). It has an estimated population of 49,997,100. In comparison, the United States covers about 3.7 million square miles (9.6 million square kilometers) and has a population of about 273 million.

England is a country within the United Kingdom (UK). This nation also includes Northern Ireland, Scotland, and Wales. The United Kingdom often is called Great Britain, or Britain. Great Britain actually is the island that includes England, Scotland, and Wales. People sometimes use the word "Britain" when talking about the UK. In comparison, the word "English" refers only to the people who live in the portion of Great Britain known as England.

Geopolitical Map of England

KEY
- ★ Capital
- • City
- ∏ Stonehenge

Fast Facts about England's Land

Area: 50,333 square miles (130,362 square kilometers)

Latitude and longitude: 53 degrees north latitude, 2 degrees west longitude at England's geographic center

Highest elevation: Scafell Pike, 3,210 feet (978 meters)

Lowest elevation: the Fens, 15 feet (4.6 meters) below sea level

Chapter 2

England's Land, Climate, and Wildlife

England's landscape consists largely of gentle, rolling hills. England is commonly divided into three main regions according to different land features and climate.

Pennines Region

The rounded uplands known as the Pennines run from Scotland about halfway down the length of England. The Pennines are also known as the Pennine Chain or Pennine Hills.

England's Lake District lies northwest of the Pennines. This small area of calm lakes and hills is one of England's most popular recreation areas. Lake Windermere, one of the area's many lakes, is the largest lake in England. It stretches 10.5 miles (17 kilometers) long and about 1 mile (1.6 kilometers)

◀ People planted trees around Tarn Hows in the Lake District to replace forests cut down long ago.

wide. Scafell Pike, England's highest point at 3,210 feet (978 meters), is in the Lake District.

The Peak District lies in the southern part of the Pennines. It contains England's first national park. The northern region of the Peak District is covered in moors and oddly shaped hills. The central and southern regions have rolling hills and green valleys.

The North York Moors lie east of the Pennines. This national park stretches across 500 square miles (1,295 square kilometers), touching the North Sea. The moors consist of low hills covered with coarse marsh grasses and low evergreen shrubs of heather.

English Lowlands

The English Lowlands region includes all land south of the Pennines and east of Wales and the Southwest Peninsula. Broad plains and gently rolling hills stretch across this region. The Lowlands region contains most of England's people, industry, and farmland.

One of the world's largest urban areas stands on the River Thames as it flows east to the North Sea. London is the capital and cultural center of the United Kingdom. Greater London has a population of more than 7 million people.

A fertile plain called the Midlands lies south of the Pennines. The Midlands plain is bordered by the Trent River to the north, the Severn River to the west, the

▼ London's Tower Bridge over the River Thames was built in 1894. Just beyond that is the Tower of London, begun in 1070. It housed kings, as well as prisoners.

> **Did you know...?**
> No place in England is more than 75 miles (121 kilometers) from the sea.

Ouse River along the east and south, and the River Thames on the south. The Midlands is a center of industry for both England and the United Kingdom. The industrial city of Birmingham is located here.

Low, flat land extends north from the Thames to The Wash, a bay of the North Sea. The Fens, a great plain that borders The Wash, is the lowest point on the island of Great Britain. Depending on the tide of the North Sea, the Fens area ranges from sea level to 15 feet (4.6 meters) below sea level.

Long lines of chalky hills and grasslands cross the land south of the Thames. At the English Channel, the hills drop sharply and form steep cliffs. The most famous of these cliffs are the white cliffs of Dover.

Southwest Peninsula

The Southwest Peninsula region lies on the southern side of the Bristol Channel, across from Wales. The peninsula is known for its white china clay, which is used to make pottery. The region consists mainly of a low plateau with some lone peaks. Dartmoor National Forest and Exmoor National Forest are highlands with granite peaks called tors. The

▼ The cliffs of Dover are a popular tourist destination in southeastern England.

Dartmoor area is famous for the wild Dartmoor ponies that live there.

The plateau ends suddenly near the coast as towering cliffs drop sharply to the sea. The peninsula ends with two smaller peninsulas shaped like a grabbing hand. One of these peninsulas is Land's End. It is England's westernmost point. The country's southernmost area is Lizard Point. It is located on the other end of the claw-shaped landmass.

Climate

England is far north of the equator. People might expect temperatures that far north to be very cold. But England experiences a mild climate. Winter temperatures average 40 degrees Fahrenheit (4.4 degrees Celsius) in England.

Warm air from the equator, called the North Atlantic Drift, flows across the Atlantic Ocean to England. This air brings warmth in winter and refreshing cool breezes during summer. Summer temperatures average about 60 degrees Fahrenheit (15.6 degrees Celsius).

Snow is rare in England. Mild fog and drizzling rain are common. The Lake District is England's wettest region, receiving an average of 130 inches (330 centimeters) of precipitation each year. The western and northern hills receive about 40 inches (102 centimeters) of rain, while the east coast receives about 20 inches (51 centimeters).

Plant Life

England does not have a great variety of native plant life. England's isolation from the European mainland kept plants from spreading there. In recent times, people have cleared the land for agriculture and other industry.

Today, forests cover just 7 percent of England's total land area. The most common trees include oak, elm, ash, and beech. The

English Gardens

The English are known as a nation of gardeners. Most English people have a garden on their property. Gardening has been a popular English pastime since Roman times. The Royal Horticultural Society, founded in 1804, has 270,000 members and sponsors the Chelsea Flower Show.

People have developed different gardening styles through the centuries. In the 1600s, people created natural parks for keeping deer and cattle. Italian and French styles influenced people to create gardens with geometric patterns.

Today, gardeners can combine foreign plants with native English flowers and shrubs. The rose, England's national flower, often plays a role in modern gardens.

▲ This English garden has geometric patterns in the center, while the outer edges are less structured.

England's Land Regions and Topography

KEY
- Pennines Region
- English Lowlands Region
- Southwestern Peninsula Region
- Plains
- Fens
- River
- Hills
- Highest Point

English oak is found in forests such as the famous Sherwood Forest.

England also has a wealth of summer wildflowers in its fields, lanes, and hedgerows. Hedgerows are rows of bushes or trees that divide fields. Heather covers the moorlands, wild roses flourish in southern England, and wild daffodils grow in the Lake District.

Wildlife

England has varied wildlife. England's forests house wild deer and ponies. Small mammals such as foxes, hares, rabbits, hedgehogs, weasels, shrews, rats, and mice are common. Some field mice and foxes have adapted to urban areas. Freshwater fish and species of marine life are numerous.

England lies along the line of bird migrations. As a result, bird life is unusually varied. England is home to nearly 230 kinds of birds and a temporary home to 200 kinds of migrating birds. A common bird in England is the red robin. The migrant cuckoo stops in England during spring. The skylark, nightingale, blackbird, and thrush are other common birds in England.

Only about six species of reptiles and six species of amphibians make their home in England. Only three species of snakes are found in England. The adder is England's only poisonous snake.

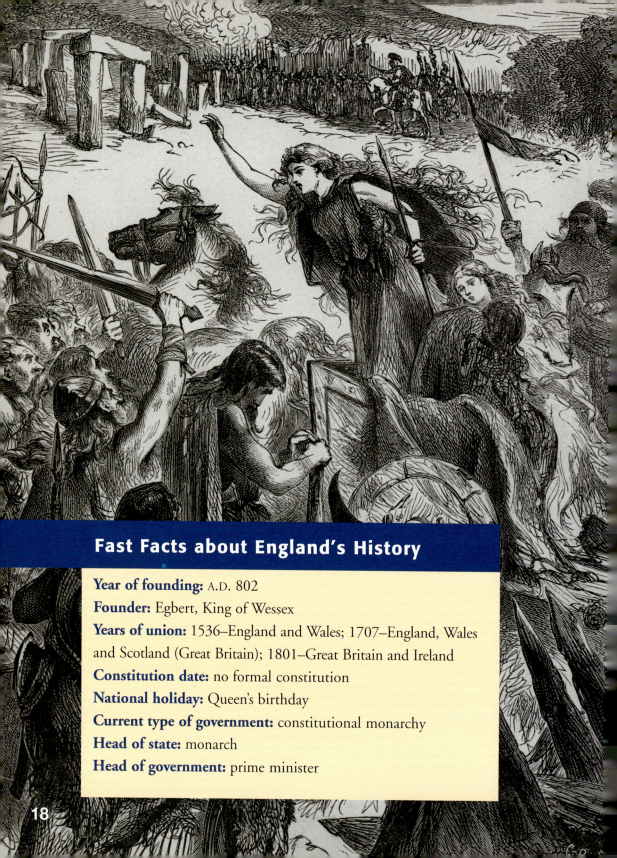

Fast Facts about England's History

Year of founding: A.D. 802

Founder: Egbert, King of Wessex

Years of union: 1536–England and Wales; 1707–England, Wales and Scotland (Great Britain); 1801–Great Britain and Ireland

Constitution date: no formal constitution

National holiday: Queen's birthday

Current type of government: constitutional monarchy

Head of state: monarch

Head of government: prime minister

Chapter 3

England's History and Government

Scientists believe people lived in England more than 8,000 years ago. In 4500 B.C., a wave of people from mainland Europe started to arrive in England. They farmed and raised livestock. They may have built stone structures such as Stonehenge.

About 650 B.C., the Celts started migrating to England from present-day France. The Celts fought against the people of the island and other Celtic tribes. But they also improved farming techniques with their use of iron plows.

Roman Rule

In A.D. 43, the Roman emperor Claudius ordered his armies to attack England. Within 40 years, the Romans controlled the southern part of Great Britain, which included present-day England and Wales.

◀ Celtic leader Boudicca led a failed revolt against the Romans during the Roman invasion.

> **Did you know…?**
> The name England comes from the Anglo-Saxon words which mean "Angle folk" or "land of the Angles."

Romans built camps, forts, and roads throughout the land. Trade increased. The port city Londinium, present-day London, grew and prospered. Romans also introduced Christianity to the area. England flourished under Roman rule for 400 years.

The Anglo-Saxon Period

In the early 400s, Roman soldiers left England to help defend Rome against invasion. The Roman soldiers had protected England from other outside invaders. England was now open to attack. Picts from Scotland and Scots from Ireland invaded. Germanic tribes of Angles, Saxons, and Jutes began to raid the island coast and established settlements in southeastern England.

The Germanic tribes continued to push their kingdoms north and west. With time, these tribal nations developed into the seven kingdoms of East Anglia, Essex, Kent, Mercia, Northumbria, Sussex, and Wessex.

From the 700s to the early 1000s, control of England switched back and forth between the Danish and Norwegian Vikings and the Anglo-Saxons. In 802, Egbert, King of Wessex, came to power. He is known as

▲ The Anglo-Saxons fought with the seagoing Vikings several times before A.D. 1000.

the first monarch of all of England because several kingdoms recognized him as the supreme leader.

Norman Rule

Harold, Earl of Wessex, became England's king in 1066. But William, the French Duke of Normandy, also claimed the English throne. On October 14, 1066, William invaded England, defeating Harold's

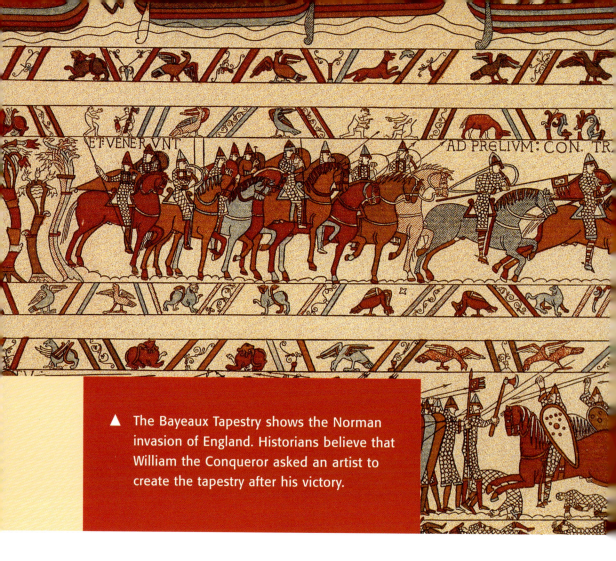

▲ The Bayeaux Tapestry shows the Norman invasion of England. Historians believe that William the Conqueror asked an artist to create the tapestry after his victory.

forces in the Battle of Hastings. Harold was killed and William was crowned king of England. He became known as William the Conqueror.

Eventually, the Normans and Anglo-Saxons in England blended their cultures and languages. The modern English language developed from their blended Germanic and French languages.

The Magna Carta

During the late 1000s and 1100s, English nobles struggled to increase their own power while the kings fought to maintain supreme authority over the country. In 1215, a group of nobles and church leaders forced the unpopular King John to sign a charter. This paper granted specific rights to the people and limited the king's power. This charter became known as the Magna Carta, or the Great Charter.

Soon, the nobles formed a council. This lawmaking body was the beginning of Parliament. In the late 1200s, Edward I established the Model Parliament. Members were nobles, churchmen, and townspeople.

The Hundred Years' War and the Wars of the Roses

When Edward III became the English king, he also tried to claim the French throne. His uncles had been French kings, so he believed he should rule both countries. This act started the Hundred Years' War (1337–1453) between England and France. As the English crown was passed down to each heir, the war with France dragged on. The war ended in 1453. England lost most of the lands on the European mainland that it had won at the start of the war.

Before the end of the Hundred Years' War, a struggle for the throne had begun between England's House of Lancaster and House of York. Lancaster's family emblem was a red rose, and York's emblem was a white rose. In 1455, the struggle between these two families became known as the Wars of the Roses (1455–1487). The Lancastrians won in the Battle of Stoke in 1487. Henry Tudor had become King Henry VII in 1485. He kept the throne as the Lancastrian king.

The Reformation and the Golden Age

King Henry VIII, Henry VII's son, successfully united England and Wales under one system of government. The two countries were joined in 1536.

Henry VIII wanted a male heir, but his wife had not given birth to a son. Henry wanted to divorce her and take a new wife. The Roman Catholic Church refused to grant the divorce.

Henry passed a law in 1584 making himself head of the church in England. This act allowed him to divorce his wife. It also led to the formation of the Protestant Church of England. Protestantism was already spreading across northern Europe. The Protestant movement was known as the Reformation.

Elizabeth I, Henry's daughter, came to the throne in 1558. Elizabeth I's rule is remembered as the Golden Age of English history. Under her rule, England

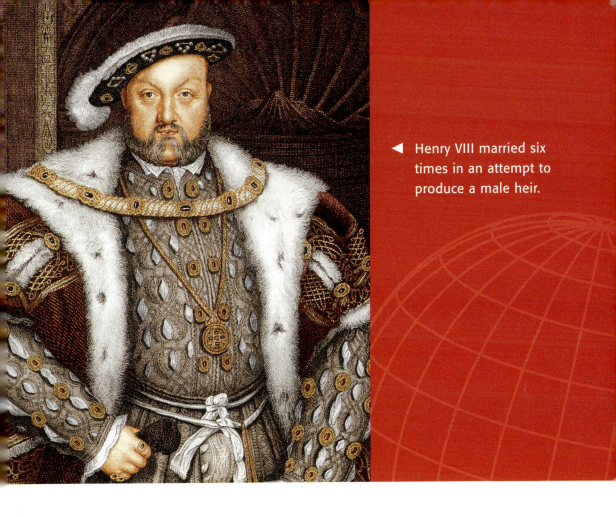

◄ Henry VIII married six times in an attempt to produce a male heir.

advanced in such areas as foreign trade, exploration, literature, and the arts.

The Bill of Rights

England briefly became a republic run by the people when Charles I was overthrown in 1649 and beheaded. The Restoration took place in 1660, when the monarchy was restored under Charles II. But authority was divided between the king and Parliament.

King James II followed Charles II as king. He favored restoring Catholicism and absolute monarchy in England. Many people did not agree with the changes James II wanted to make. Parliament invited the Dutch King William III, who was married to Charles II's daughter Mary, to invade England. King William drove James II out of England in 1688.

This period of English history is known as the Glorious Revolution. It marked the time when Parliament established the right to approve or disapprove the monarchs who would rule England. In 1689, Parliament passed the Bill of Rights, which guaranteed the people certain basic civil rights. The Bill of Rights also prevented the monarch from performing some acts without Parliament's approval. After accepting the terms of the Bill of Rights, William and Mary became joint rulers of England.

In 1707, England and Wales joined with Scotland in the Act of Union. This new country was called the Kingdom of Great Britain.

The Richest Country in the World

During the 1600s and 1700s, England claimed territory all over the world. It had 13 colonies in America and large sugar farms in the West Indies. It ran a profitable slave trade between Africa and its colonies in North America. England also had trading

▲ The English Parliament forced William III to sign the Bill of Rights before he could take the English throne.

interests in India and the Far East. It was fast becoming the richest country in the world.

The Industrial Revolution during the 1700s and 1800s helped contribute to England's wealth. During the Industrial Revolution, people invented machines that replaced hand labor. Factory systems developed, and agricultural techniques improved. Better, faster production meant more goods to trade. People built

▲ During the Industrial Revolution, machines made production faster and cheaper.

roads, canals, and railways to meet the need for better trade routes. England increased its trade with its colonies and other countries.

Trouble with Ireland and France

For centuries, England had governed Ireland. While the majority of the English were Protestants, most Irish were Roman Catholics. The people of Ireland rebelled against English rule in 1798. British leaders responded by making Ireland part of Britain. In 1801, the English Parliament passed an Act of Union that created the United Kingdom of Great Britain and Ireland.

France, under the command of Napoleon Bonaparte, conquered much of the European continent. In 1803, he began a plan to invade Britain. But in 1805, Napoleon suffered a devastating defeat to the British in the Battle of Trafalgar. Still, he attacked other European areas and controlled most of Europe by 1812. Napoleon was finally defeated in 1815 in the Battle of Waterloo.

From 1837 to 1901, Queen Victoria ruled the UK. Her reign, known as the Victorian Age, was the longest in British history. The British Empire reached its height. Its holdings included about one-quarter of the world's land as well as about one-quarter of the world's people.

World Wars and Irish Independence

The Allied Powers of the UK, France, and Russia fought the Central Powers of Austria-Hungary and Germany during World War I (1914–1918). Although the Allied Powers won, the UK suffered the loss of nearly 750,000 troops in the war. The nation's position as a world power was uncertain. The country was swept into an economic depression. Many people were unemployed.

After World War I, Britain's relationship with Ireland became explosive. In 1919, Irish leaders declared Ireland independent of Britain. Irish rebels fought Britain. In 1921, southern Ireland became a British territory called the Irish Free State. It was a self-governing member of the British Empire. Northern Ireland remained a part of the United Kingdom.

World War II (1939–1945) began in September 1939. The Axis powers of Germany and Italy had invaded several countries in Europe. The UK and France, the Allies, declared war on the Axis powers. They tried to drive out the Axis Powers and prevent further invasions.

During this war, England withstood many bombings by German warplanes. The Allies eventually included the UK, the United States, the Soviet Union, and nearly 50 other nations. Japan eventually joined the Axis powers. The Allies finally defeated the Axis Powers in 1945. About 360,000 British people died in the war. Bombs had destroyed great sections of London and other cities. The UK had spent a huge amount of money on the war. It had no money to buy goods or rebuild.

Lost Colonies

Before World War II, Britain had already started to lose control over its colonies around the world. By 1931, Britain had granted self-government to Australia,

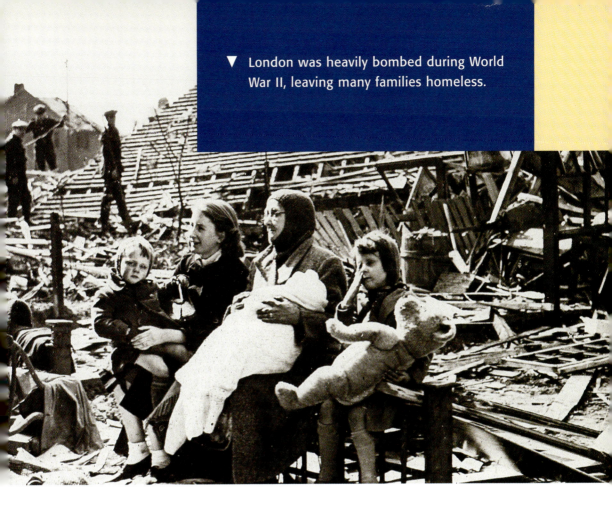

▼ London was heavily bombed during World War II, leaving many families homeless.

Canada, the Irish Free State, New Zealand, Newfoundland, and South Africa.

After World War II, the UK granted independence to most of its colonies. In 1947, India and Pakistan became independent, self-governing nations within the Commonwealth. The Irish Free State declared itself the independent Republic of Ireland and left the Commonwealth in 1949. Many African colonies also won their independence from Britain.

▼ Peace walls were constructed in Belfast, Northern Ireland, to try to stop violence between Catholics and Protestants.

England Today

In 1973, the United Kingdom entered the European Union (EU). Currently, 15 European countries make up this union. It builds economic and social policy for its member countries in order to strengthen the European market and community. In 1999, the EU introduced a new currency called the euro. The United Kingdom has not adopted this currency.

Tension in Northern Ireland continues to affect the United Kingdom. Rioting and violence have occurred for decades between Catholics and Protestants in Northern Ireland. In 1998, the United Kingdom responded by forming a government in which Catholics and Protestants share power in Northern Ireland. Occasional fighting continues.

Government

England is one of four divisions that make up the United Kingdom. The United Kingdom's Parliament runs England's day-to-day affairs.

The United Kingdom is a constitutional monarchy. The nation does not have a formal constitution. The country is governed by laws passed by Parliament, historic documents such as the Magna Carta, and British common law.

In the executive branch of government, the monarch rules as head of state. The monarch's duties are mostly ceremonial. The prime minister is the head of government. The leader of the majority party in the House of Commons usually becomes prime minister. The prime minister selects ministers to make up the Cabinet. The Cabinet helps the prime minister oversee the government and develop policy to introduce to Parliament.

The legislative branch is made up of Parliament. Parliament makes laws for the United Kingdom. It is made up of the House of Commons and the House of Lords. The House of Lords is made up of nobility who inherit their seats. They hold nearly 1,200 seats in Parliament, but their power is limited.

The House of Commons, with 659 elected members, is more powerful than the House of Lords. Members represent the four regions that make up the United Kingdom. England sends 529 elected officials to the House of Commons. The remaining members are elected from voting districts in Wales, Scotland, and Northern Ireland. Citizens elect members of the House of Commons in a national election held at least every five years. United Kingdom citizens 18 years old or older may vote.

England and Wales share one court system. Some courts hear criminal cases while others handle only civil

▼ The Lord Chancellor of the House of Lords (left) wears the wig common to all who serve in the House of Lords. Members of the House of Commons do not wear wigs.

cases. Court decisions can be appealed to higher courts. The House of Lords is the highest court of appeal.

Locally, England is divided into several government units such as counties and metropolitan districts. Counties are further divided into districts called shires. Each government unit has its own elected council that handles local matters such as education, housing, and road construction.

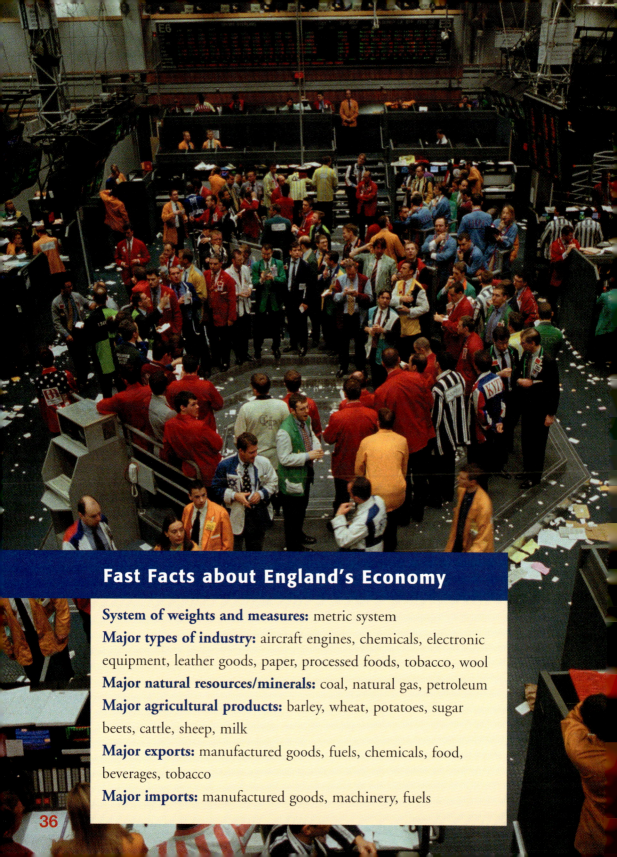

Fast Facts about England's Economy

System of weights and measures: metric system
Major types of industry: aircraft engines, chemicals, electronic equipment, leather goods, paper, processed foods, tobacco, wool
Major natural resources/minerals: coal, natural gas, petroleum
Major agricultural products: barley, wheat, potatoes, sugar beets, cattle, sheep, milk
Major exports: manufactured goods, fuels, chemicals, food, beverages, tobacco
Major imports: manufactured goods, machinery, fuels

Chapter 4

England's Economy

England's excellent harbors and ideal location on the busy North Atlantic shipping lanes make it a natural center of trade. Trade has been important to England's economy for hundreds of years. The United Kingdom is a member of the EU, the world's largest established trading group. The UK is the fourth largest trading nation in the world.

Service Industries

England's economy has experienced its fastest growth in service jobs. The number of people employed in service positions has more than doubled in the last 40 years. Today, 75 percent of employees work in service areas. These jobs are in health services, education, government, communications, trade, financial services, and other personal services.

◀ London's stock exchange is part of England's large financial service industry.

England's banking and insurance businesses are its most important service industries. London is an international financial center. The London Stock Exchange is one of the world's busiest stock exchanges. Millions of company shares are bought and sold there every day. Lloyd's of London is a famous worldwide insurance company.

Manufacturing, Mining, and Energy

Most of the UK's exports are goods manufactured in England. The nation has been a leader in manufacturing since the beginning of the Industrial Revolution in the 1700s. Today, people who hold manufacturing jobs make up nearly one-fifth of the nation's workforce.

England's manufacturing workforce produces chemicals, clothing, electronic equipment, aircraft engines, fabricated steel products, leather goods, paper, processed foods, tobacco, and textiles. The UK also is a leader in printing and publishing.

The UK has large coal, natural gas, and oil reserves. England ranks as a major coal producer with its largest coal fields extending along both sides of the Pennines into the Midlands. For many years, the UK's coal resources powered factories and heated homes.

England's Industries and Natural Resources

KEY
- coal
- fish
- fruit
- grain
- livestock
- manufacturing
- oil
- potatoes

Less coal is mined today because people use other energy sources such as oil, natural gas, and nuclear power. Oil and natural gas deposits lie east of Great Britain in the North Sea. Other oil deposits are in the English Channel.

Agriculture and Fishing

Agriculture and fishing employ less than 2 percent of the nation's workers. Farming in Great Britain is highly mechanized and efficient. As proof, the tiny agricultural workforce farms nearly 80 percent of Britain's land and provides 60 percent of the nation's food needs.

Dairy and cattle farming produce England's major agriculture products of milk and beef. Other chief products include barley, chicken and eggs, fruits, potatoes, mutton and wool, sugar beets, and wheat.

England's shallow coastal waters are an excellent source of cod, haddock, and mackerel. The nation's two main fishing ports are Kingston upon Hull on the North Sea coast and Fleetwood on the Irish Sea coast.

Transportation

England has a wide variety of transportation systems. Highways link the nation's industrial centers. Car

▲ Hedgerows and stone walls have divided England's fields for hundreds of years.

> **Did you know...?**
> British scientist Sir Alexander Fleming discovered penicillin in 1928. Penicillin was the first antibiotic used successfully to treat serious diseases in human beings.

travel is the most popular type of transportation. Most people age 17 or older are eligible for a driver's license.

England has good passenger and freight train transportation. In 1994, a railway tunnel linking the United Kingdom and France opened beneath the English Channel. Called the "Chunnel," it is 31 miles (50 kilometers) from its entrance in England to its entrance in France. Nearly 24 of those miles (39 kilometers) are underwater. The Chunnel carries freight trains, high-speed passenger trains, and shuttle trains.

England's island location has compelled it to build upon its waterways. England has many important ports, including London, Southampton, and Liverpool. In the 1800s, England developed a widespread inland waterway system of rivers and canals. Today, these waterways are used primarily for recreation. Ferryboats carry passengers across the English Channel between England and France.

England's Money

England's currency is the pound sterling. One pound equals 100 pence.

Currency exchange rates change every day. In 2002, .71 English pounds equaled 1 U.S. dollar and .44 English pounds equaled 1 Canadian dollar.

2 pound coin

2 pence coin

1 pound coin

10 pound note

10 pound note

Fast Facts about England's People

Population distribution: urban—95 percent; rural—5 percent
Official language: English
Population growth rate: 0.23 percent (United Kingdom)
Life expectancy: male—75 years; female—81 years; total population—78 years (United Kingdom)
Literacy rate: 99 percent of people in the UK age 15 and older who have completed five or more years of schooling can read

Chapter 5

England's People, Culture, and Daily Life

The English have made major contributions to the world in areas of science, law, and the arts. The English language is the second most widely spoken native language in the world.

Culture, Language, and Religion

As people came to England, they brought their own traditions and speech. The Celts were the first of many people to shape the English culture. Romans, Angles, Saxons, Jutes, Danes, and Normans followed. The English language, which developed mainly from the Anglo-Saxon and Norman-French languages, is the official language of the United Kingdom. Many immigrants also speak their native languages.

For centuries, people from around the world have flocked to England and the United Kingdom. Before

◀ London's Covent Garden features shops, street performers, and a flea market.

▼ These children immigrated to England in 1968. Starting in the 1950s, many Asian people immigrated to England.

and after World War II, Europeans poured into England to escape troubles in their homelands. Since the 1950s, many immigrants have come to England from countries in Asia and the West Indies. During the 1960s and 1970s, immigrants arrived from Africa. Still, nonwhite minority groups make up little more than 6 percent of the ethnic minority population.

The Church of England, or Anglican Church, is the official church in England. It has about 27 million members. The British monarch is the Anglican church's worldly head and must belong to it. Other English people have the freedom to worship as they choose.

> **Did you know...?**
> People cannot legally own guns in England. Police officers do not even carry guns unless they have special permission.

Many English people belong to Protestant churches such as the Baptist, Methodist, and United Reformed churches. England has a population of about 4 million Roman Catholics. England also has one of the largest Jewish populations in Europe. Others in England practice Islam, Buddhism, Hinduism, and other religions.

Living Conditions

Until the mid-1800s, most people in England lived in the countryside. But during the Industrial Revolution, huge numbers of people moved to cities and towns to work in factories, mines, and mills.

Today, England is densely populated. About 95 percent of its people live in urban areas. England's cities are modern business and entertainment centers. Suburban areas of tidy houses and well-kept gardens rim the edges of the cities.

As in cities throughout the world, housing shortages force the poorest people into the most undesirable areas. In England, many members of minority groups live in crowded inner-city housing. Unemployment, traffic, and air pollution are other problems that affect life in England's urban areas.

About 5 percent of England's people live in rural areas in southwestern England, eastern England, and the northern Pennines. Some rural people live in small towns or country villages. Others live in homes far from any neighbors. Farming is an important activity in these rural areas.

English people's lifestyles have changed in the past century. Parents usually have fewer children than they did 100 years ago. Single parents head more than 25 percent of English households. Women make up 45 percent of the labor market. Many women delay having children until they are age 30 or older.

Education

Education is a top priority in England and throughout the United Kingdom. About 99 percent of people age 15 or older who have had 5 years of schooling can read and write. The Department for Education and Skills supervises England's school system. The system requires all children between the ages of 5 and 16 to attend school.

▲ Houses in England's cities, like these in Lancaster, often are crowded close together.

About 90 percent of England's students go to schools supported entirely or partly by public funds. The remaining 10 percent attend private schools. Parents must pay fees to have their children attend private schools. Most of these places are boarding schools for boys. The students live at the school during the school term. Private schools tend to have smaller class sizes and higher levels of accomplishment.

Learn British Slang

People in England often use different words for everyday things than people in the United States do.

In England:	In the United States:
biscuit	cookie
bobby	police officer
bonnet	hood of a car
boot	trunk of a car
cheers	thank you, goodbye
chips	french fries
flat	apartment
joint of meat	roast
lift	elevator
lorry	truck
petrol	gasoline
underground	subway

Children in England go to elementary school from ages 5 to 11. They then follow a course of study that prepares them for college, the workplace, or vocational training. Although they are not required to do so, students may continue their high school education past age 16.

Students may enter England's university system after high school. England's universities include two of the most famous universities in the world, Oxford and Cambridge. The University of London is England's largest traditional university. It has about 60,000 students.

Sports and Leisure

People enjoy various indoor and outdoor activities in England. Many people visit the local pub to eat and drink, chat with friends, or play darts. Many people take long hikes through the countryside or work in their gardens.

Other people like to take part in organized sports. Football, known as soccer in the United States, is England's most popular sport. Cricket, which is played with a bat and ball, is another popular sport in England. Almost all towns and villages have cricket teams. Rugby is similar to American football. It is played throughout England from late summer to late spring.

Other favorite sports include golf, horse racing, rowing, sailing, swimming, and tennis. People enjoy fox hunting, horseback riding, and fishing throughout the English countryside.

Food

Many traditional English dishes are simple. Meals often include roasted and grilled meats. A roast of beef, pork, or lamb, called a joint, is the typical main dish for Sunday dinners. The joint usually is served with roasted or boiled potatoes, a vegetable, and a dessert. Dessert often consists of a fruit pie topped with hot custard sauce. Yorkshire pudding, a batter cake baked in meat fat, is often served with beef. Cooks often serve cabbage, brussels sprouts, cauliflower, peas, and carrots because these vegetables are easy to grow in England's climate.

Cooks serve other popular English dishes. Steak and kidney pie is a stew made of beef and beef kidneys topped by a pastry crust. Shepherd's pie is a casserole of ground meat and mashed potatoes. Bangers and mash is a dish of thick sausages served with mashed potatoes. Fish and chips are a favorite lunch. People in the United States call chips "french fries." Tea with milk is served at 4:00 in the afternoon and eaten with cookies, commonly called biscuits.

Treacle Tart

This lemon tart can be served as a dessert. Please ask an adult to help you with this recipe.

What You Need

2 unbaked pie crusts
6 tablespoons (90 mL) golden syrup (may substitute light molasses or honey)
2 ounces (55 grams) fresh white bread crumbs
finely grated rind of 1 lemon
1 teaspoon (5 mL) lemon juice

pie pan
measuring spoons
measuring cups
saucepan
knife
pot holders
cooling rack

What You Do

1. Line pie pan with dough of one unbaked pie crust.
2. Combine 6 tablespoons syrup, 2 ounces bread crumbs, lemon rind, and 1 teaspoon lemon juice in saucepan. Heat on low until mixture is just melted.
3. Pour the syrup mixture into the prepared pie crust.
4. Cut remaining crust into long, narrow strips.
5. Arrange strips in a lattice (woven) pattern over the filling.
6. Bake in oven at 400° Fahrenheit (200° Celsius) for 25 to 30 minutes or until the pastry is slightly browned.
7. Cut the pastry into squares or wedges and serve hot or cold.

Makes 8 servings.

Art and Literature

Many famous artists were born in England. The English composer William Byrd is known for the church music he wrote. Henry Purcell is considered one of England's greatest classical composers. In modern times, the Beatles and the Rolling Stones have had an enormous influence on the development of rock music.

English artists have created collectible furniture and china. Furniture collectors treasure the works of the English furniture maker Thomas Chippendale. Josiah Wedgwood and Josiah Spode made chinaware during the 1700s. Wedgwood and Spode pottery remains one of the United Kingdom's most important exports.

Arguably, England's greatest artists have been writers such as Geoffrey Chaucer, Charles Dickens, and William Shakespeare. Students throughout the world study Shakespeare's plays, such as *Romeo and Juliet* and *Hamlet*.

Holidays and Celebrations

England recognizes a range of holidays. Often the celebrations focus on functions of the monarch. For example, the monarch reviews the royal troops in June during "Trooping the Colour."

▼ The Queen reviews her troops during "Trooping the Colour."

People celebrate Guy Fawkes Day on November 5. In 1605, Guy Fawkes led a plot to blow up the Parliament building, but the plot failed. People celebrate this day with fireworks. They also light bonfires and set fire to dummies representing Guy Fawkes.

Christians celebrate traditional Christian holidays. Good Friday and Easter Sunday are celebrated in the spring and Christmas on December 25.

▲ English Royal Guards stand silently at the head of Buckingham Palace. The guards are trained to ignore distractions. Tourists often try to make the guards smile or move.

England's National Symbols

◀ **England's Flag**
The Union Jack is the official flag of the United Kingdom. It is red, white, and blue with a red cross through the center. England has no official flag, but the flag called St. George's Cross has been used for centuries. It consists of a white background and a red cross like the Union Jack.

◀ **England's Coat of Arms**
England uses Great Britain's coat of arms, which features lions and a unicorn.

Other National Symbols

National anthem: "God Save the Queen"
National flower: rose
National animal symbol: lion

Timeline

1283 England conquers Wales.

A.D. 43 Roman armies invade England.

1215 King John signs the Magna Carta.

1455–1487 The Wars of the Roses take place between English houses of Lancaster and York.

1660 Parliament restores the monarchy, known as the Restoration.

B.C. A.D. 1000   1500

6,000 B.C. The first people arrive in England.

1066 William the Conqueror takes the English crown in the Battle of Hastings.

1337–1453 The Hundred Years' War takes place between England and France.

1536 An Act of Union is passed that unites England and Wales.

1649 People revolt against the monarchy; England briefly becomes a republic.

1688
The Glorious Revolution ends James II's rule.

1949
Ireland declares independence; the UK becomes the United Kingdom of Great Britain and Northern Ireland.

1689
Parliament passes the Bill of Rights.

1815
Britain defeats France in the Napoleonic Wars.

1939–1945
World War II

1994
The Channel Tunnel opens between England and France.

1700 — **1900** — **2000**

1707
An Act of Union unites England, Wales, and Scotland; they become the Kingdom of Great Britain.

1801
Ireland joins the Kingdom of Great Britain; they become the United Kingdom of Great Britain and Ireland.

1914–1918
World War I

1998
A peace accord is signed in Northern Ireland.

1973
The UK becomes a member of the European Union.

Words to Know

civil rights (SIV-il RITES)—individual rights that all people of a society have to freedom and equal treatment under the law

hedgerow (HEJ-roh)—narrow strips of trees and flowers that often divide fields

heir (AIR)—someone who has been or will be left something of great value such as a position of royalty

invade (in-VADE)—to send armed forces into another country in order to take it over

migration (mye-GRAY-shuhn)—the act of moving from one region or place to another region or place to live

moor (MOR)—open, rolling land covered with coarse marsh grasses and low evergreen shrubs of heather

peninsula (puh-NIN-suh-luh)—a piece of land that sticks out from a larger landmass and is almost completely surrounded by water

plateau (pla-TOH)—an area of high, flat land

Protestant (PROT-uh-stuhnt)—a Christian who does not belong to the Roman Catholic or the Orthodox church

pub (PUHB)—a bar that serves alcohol and sometimes food

tor (TOR)—a high hill of sharp granite

To Learn More

Blashfield, Jean F. *England.* Enchantment of the World. Second Series. New York: Children's Press, 1997.

Hatt, Christine. *London.* World Cities. Mankato, Minn.: Thameside Press, 2000.

Lace, William W. *England.* Modern Nations of the World. San Diego: Lucent Books, 1997.

Lyle, Garry. *England.* Major World Nations. Philadelphia: Chelsea House Publishers, 2000.

Useful Addresses

British High Commission
80 Elgin Street
Ottawa, ON K1P 5K7
Canada

Embassy of the United Kingdom in the United States
3100 Massachusetts Avenue NW
Washington, DC 20008

Internet Sites

Britain USA
http://britainusa.com
Information and news from the British Embassy in the United States

CIA—The World Factbook—United Kingdom
http://www.odci.gov/cia/publications/factbook/geos/uk.html
Information from the U.S. Central Intelligence Agency

National Statistics
http://www.statistics.gov.uk
The official government site of UK vital statistics

VisitBritain
http://www.visitbritain.com
The official Web site of the British Tourist Authority

▲ This worker harvests lavender from a large field in England. England is famous for this aromatic flower.

Index

Act of Union
    1536 (Wales), 24
    1707 (Scotland), 26
    1801 (Ireland), 29
agriculture, 10, 14, 19, 27, 40, 48, 63
Anglican Church, 24, 47
Anglo-Saxons, 20–21, 22, 45
animals. See wildlife
art, 25, 54

Battle of Hastings, 22
Battle of Trafalgar, 29
Battle of Waterloo, 29
Bill of Rights, 26, 27
Bonaparte, Napoleon, 29

Celts, 19, 45
Charles I, 25
Charles II, 25, 26
Christianity, 20, 55
Church of England. See Anglican Church
climate, 9, 14, 52
colonies, 26–27, 28, 30–31
constitution, 33

Dover, cliffs of, 12, 13

education, 35, 37, 48–49, 51
Egbert, 20–21
Elizabeth I, 24–25
English Channel, 6, 12, 40, 42
ethnic groups, 45–46
European Union (EU), 33, 37

farming. See agriculture
Fens, 12
fishing, 40, 52
fog, 14
food, 38, 40, 52, 53
France, 19, 23, 29, 30, 42

Glorious Revolution, 26
Golden Age, 24
government, 24, 30, 33–35, 37
    executive branch, 34
    judicial branch. See judicial system
    legislative branch, 34

Harold I, 21–22
hedgerow, 17, 41
Henry VIII, 24, 25
holidays, 54–55
housing, 35, 47–48, 49
Hundred Years' War, 23–24

Industrial Revolution, 27–28, 38, 47
industry, 10, 12, 14, 39
Ireland, 6, 20, 28–29, 30, 31
Irish Sea, 6, 40

James II, 26
judicial system, 34–35

Lake District, 9–10, 14, 17
Lake Windermere, 9–10
language, 22, 45, 50
London, 10, 11, 20, 30, 31, 37, 38, 42, 45

Magna Carta, 23, 33
manufacturing, 38
Midlands, 10, 12, 38
mining, 38, 40

natural resources, 38, 39, 40
Normans, 21–22, 45
North Atlantic Drift, 14
Northern Ireland, 6, 30, 32, 33, 34
North Sea, 6, 10, 12, 40

Parliament, 23, 25, 26, 27, 29, 33, 34
    House of Commons, 34, 35
    House of Lords, 34, 35
Peak District, 10
Pennines, 9, 10, 38, 48
plain, 10, 12
plant life, 14, 15, 17
precipitation, 14

rainfall. See precipitation
Reformation, 24
religion, 47, 55
River Thames, 10, 11, 12
Roman Catholic Church, 24, 26, 47
Romans, 19–20, 45

Scafell Pike, 10
Scotland, 6, 9, 20, 26, 34
service industry, 37–38
sports, 51–52
Stonehenge, 5, 19

temperature, 14
transportation, 40, 42

Victoria, 29
Victorian Age, 29
Vikings, 20, 21

Wales, 6, 10, 12, 19, 24, 26, 34–35
Wars of the Roses, 24
Wash, The, 12
wildlife, 17
William III, 26, 27
William the Conqueror, 21–22
World War I, 29–30
World War II, 30, 31, 46